CHEDDAR & CHEESES

By
Sherri Eldridge

Illustrations by
Rob Groves

Cheddar & Cheeses

Copyright 1998 Harvest Hill Press

All rights reserved. Neither this book nor any portion of this book may be reproduced in any form without the written permission of Harvest Hill Press.

Published by:
Harvest Hill Press
Post Office Box 55
Salisbury Cove, Maine 04672
207-288-8900

ISBN: 1-886862-30-3

First printing: August 1998
Second printing: May 1999

PRINTED IN THE UNITED STATES
ON ACID-FREE PAPER

The recipes in this book were created with the goal of reducing fat, calories, cholesterol and sodium. They also present a variety of fresh healthy foods, to be prepared with love and eaten with pleasure.

CREDITS:

Cover cotton border gratefully used as a courtesy of:
Julie Ingleman

Cover Design, Layout and Typesetting: Sherri Eldridge

Front Cover Watercolor and Text Line Art: Robert Groves

Text Typesetting and Proofreading: Bill Eldridge

PREFACE

The first written record of cheese belongs to the Sumerians, around 4,000 BC. There are references to cheese throughout the Old Testament and the Greeks even had a god of cheese - Aristaeus. The Romans loved cheese so much that the rich had special kitchens whose only purpose was to make cheese. From the Greek and Roman languages came the Western World's names for cheese. From Greek *formos* came Italian *formaggio* and French *fromage*. From Latin *caseus* came German *käse*, Irish *cais*, Spanish *queso* and English *chese*.

Until the Middle Ages, cheese production was simple. It was fresh like cottage cheese, hard-pressed like Parmesan, or veined like Roquefort. During the Middle Ages monks in monasteries throughout Europe experimented and developed most of the fine cheeses of today, with the center of this development revolving around France.

Cheese is made throughout the world. In the USA, the states of Vermont, New York, Wisconsin and Oregon are known for their fine Cheddars and also Coon, Colby, Monterey Jack and Liederkranz. England is the home of many great Cheddars. France is famous for its double and triple creams, goat cheeses and Roquefort. Holland has Gouda and Edam. Scandinavia produces specialty blues. Italy is known for Parmesan and fresh mozzarella. Greece has feta, and Switzerland is known for Gruyère.

CONTENTS

Marvelous Muenster Omelette	7
Oatmeal and Cheese Custard	8
Cheddar Scones	9
Jalapeño Cheese Biscuits	10
Parmesan Herb Bread	11
A Cheese-Making Primer	12
Tomato, Basil & Pea Quiche	13
Fondue	14
Cheddar Chutney	15
Jalapeño Bites	15
Lemon Chèvre	16
Roquefort Dressing	16
Selecting and Storing Cheeses	17
Artichoke Dip	18
Cucumber & Feta Marinade	18
Strawberry Stilton Salad	19
Broccoli Cheddar Soup	20
Cheddar Mornay Flounder	21
Scallops with Mushrooms au Gratin	22
The Cheese Chart	24
Risotto Parmesan	25
Cheesy Macaroni with Roasted Vegetables	26
Onion Pie	27
Gorgonzola Potatoes	28
Brie Pudding with Fruit Sauce	29
Blueberry Cheesecake	30
Tiramisu Parfaits	31

CHEDDAR & CHEESES

Marvelous Muenster Omelette

1 egg
3 egg whites
¼ teaspoon pepper
1 teaspoon butter
3 tablespoons lowfat grated Muenster
1 teaspoon chopped parsley

Serving: 1/2 Recipe
Protein: 9 gm
Carbs: 1 gm
Sodium: 174 mg
Calories: 112
Fat: 7.5 gm
Cholesterol: 122 mg
Calcium: 93 mg

SERVES 2

Beat egg, egg whites and pepper.

Spray an 8-inch omelette pan with non-stick oil. Over high heat, melt butter in pan. When butter foams, pour eggs into pan and spread evenly with spatula. Cook 1 minute, then spread cheese over omelette. While shaking pan at slight angle, use spatula to fold omelette in half with cheese inside. Cook another minute or two, until omelette feels spongy, but still moist. Sprinkle with parsley, serve immediately.

CHEDDAR & CHEESES

Oatmeal and Cheese Custard

2 eggs
3 egg whites
1½ cups skim milk
¾ cup rolled oats
½ cup grated lowfat
   Monterey Jack cheese
½ cup shredded wheat cereal

SERVES 4

Preheat oven to 350°. Spray a 1½-quart casserole dish with nonstick oil.

In a mixing bowl, beat eggs into milk. Stir in oats and cheese. Pour mixture into casserole dish. Crush shredded wheat evenly over top. Bake 40 minutes or until custard is set. Serve hot.

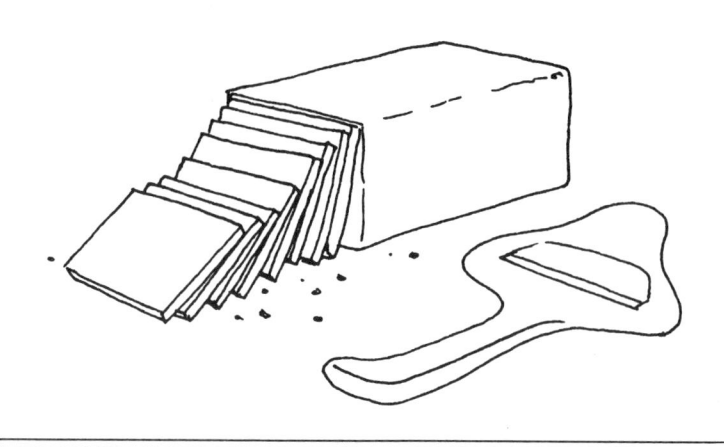

Serving: 1/4 Recipe
Protein: 16 gm
Carbs: 20 gm
Sodium: 165 mg
Calories: 187
Fat: 5 gm
Cholesterol: 112 mg
Calcium: 248 mg

CHEDDAR & CHEESES

Cheddar Scones

1 cup rolled oats
1 cup unbleached flour
1 tablespoon baking powder
1 teaspoon baking soda
½ tablespoon canola oil
1 teaspoon brown mustard
½ cup grated lowfat
   Cheddar cheese
1 cup lowfat buttermilk

Serving: 1 Scone
Protein: 7 gm
Carbs: 21 gm
Sodium: 399 mg

Calories: 141
Fat: 3.5 gm
Cholesterol: 4 mg
Calcium: 169 mg

SERVES 8

Preheat oven to 400°. Spray a heavy baking sheet with nonstick oil.

Stir oats, flour, baking powder and baking soda together in a mixing bowl. Using a pastry cutter, cut oil and mustard into mixture. Stir in grated cheese. Mix buttermilk into dough. On a board dusted with flour, knead dough 6 times. Divide in half and shape each half into a circle about ¼ inch thick. Use a sharp knife to quarter each circle into 4 wedges. Place wedges at least 1 inch apart on a baking sheet. Bake until lightly colored, about 15-20 minutes.

CHEDDAR & CHEESES

Jalapeño Cheese Biscuits

2 cups all-purpose flour
1 teaspoon sugar
pinch of salt
2 tablespoons baking powder
½ teaspoon dried oregano
pinch of crushed fennel seeds
3 tablespoons canola oil
¾ cup skim milk
1 cup grated lowfat Monterey Jack cheese
2 tablespoons chopped jalapeño peppers

Serving: 1 Biscuit
Protein: 6 gm
Carbs: 17 gm
Sodium: 248 mg
Calories: 131
Fat: 4.5 gm
Cholesterol: 3 mg
Calcium: 178 mg

MAKES 12 BISCUITS

Preheat oven to 425°. Spray a heavy baking sheet with nonstick oil.

Mix together all dry ingredients. With a fork, stir in oil, milk, cheese and peppers until flour is just moistened. Knead dough 30 seconds on floured board, then pat out dough to a 1-inch thickness. Use a drinking glass to cut into 2-inch rounds. Arrange them at least 1 inch apart on the baking sheet. Bake 15 minutes, or until puffed and golden. Cool on a wire rack.

CHEDDAR & CHEESES

Parmesan Herb Bread

1 cup warm water
2 pkgs. active dry yeast
1 teaspoon sugar
5 cups all-purpose flour
1 cup plain nonfat yogurt
½ cup grated Parmesan cheese
2 tablespoons canola oil
½ teaspoon salt
¾ teaspoon dried basil
½ teaspoon garlic powder

Serving: 1 Slice
Protein: 4 gm
Carbs: 21 gm
Sodium: 82 mg

Calories: 122
Fat: 2 gm
Cholesterol: 2 mg
Calcium: 45 mg

MAKES 2 LOAVES

Preheat oven to 350°. Spray two 5" x 9" bread pans with nonstick oil.

Combine water, yeast and sugar in a mixing bowl and let sit 5 minutes. Add 2 cups flour and remaining ingredients. Stir well. Add another 2¼ cups flour, stir well, then knead in remaining flour. Knead until smooth and elastic.

Place dough in a large bowl that has been sprayed with nonstick oil, turning to coat all sides, then cover. Let rise in a warm place until double in bulk. Punch down dough, knead 2 minutes. Divide in half, shape into loaves and let rise in pans until double in bulk. Bake for 45 minutes or until loaves sound hollow when tapped. Remove from pans and cool. To store, wrap in aluminum foil and freeze. To defrost, thaw then reheat in foil at 300° for 15 minutes.

CHEDDAR & CHEESES

A Cheese Making Primer

All cheese is made from milk, whether from cows, sheep, goats, buffalo, reindeer, or yaks. To the fresh milk, a bacteria culture is added to separate the milk into curds and whey. Curds are white milky lumps with the consistency of custard, and whey is the thin liquid left after the curds form. The curds are then cut into small pieces, processed and aged. While this general description fits all cheese making, any small variation results in a different cheese.

It all starts with the milk. Morning milk differs from afternoon. What the animal eats affects the taste. How much heat is applied during separation, as well as the size and method of cutting the curds, all result in different cheeses. The curds can be pressed, drained, ripened warm or cool, for days or years, and even turned during the ripening process. They can be inoculated with a mold or rubbed with brandy, salt or herbs. These combinations result in the multitude of cheeses produced throughout the world.

Cheeses have some names with which we are very familiar, and some are known only to a few local residents. Naming cheeses generally follows six major rules: the town where they were first produced or marketed, an ingredient, the shape, the milk from which it is made, the name of the maker, or the ecclesiastical names bestowed by the monks on their creations.

CHEDDAR & CHEESES

Tomato, Basil & Pea Quiche

SERVES 8

- 1½ cups nonfat cracker crumbs
- 2 tablespoons canola oil
- 2 tablespoons skim milk
- 5 peeled whole tomatoes
- 1 tablespoon grated onion
- 1 teaspoon canola oil
- ¾ cup fresh sweet peas
- 2 eggs, beaten
- 2 egg whites, beaten
- 1 cup skim milk
- 1 tablespoon fresh basil
- 1 teaspoon Worcestershire
- ¾ cup grated lowfat Swiss Lorraine cheese

Preheat oven to 375°. Spray a 9-inch pie pan with nonstick oil.

Put cracker crumbs in a mixing bowl. Sprinkle oil and milk over crumbs, then distribute moisture with a fork. Press crumbs into pie pan bottom and up the sides. Bake 5 minutes.

Cut tomatoes into bite-sized pieces, drain in sieve 15 minutes, then gently press out liquid. Sauté onions in oil until nearly clear. Steam peas 5 minutes. Combine tomatoes, onions, peas and all remaining ingredients in a mixing bowl. Pour into prepared pie shell. Bake 30 minutes or until golden brown.

Serving: 1 Piece
Protein: 10 gm
Carbs: 25 gm
Sodium: 87 mg

Calories: 191
Fat: 6 gm
Cholesterol: 57 mg
Calcium: 163 mg

CHEDDAR & CHEESES

Fondue

½ lb. lowfat Swiss cheese
3 oz. Gruyère cheese
1 teaspoon cornstarch
1 teaspoon nutmeg
3 tablespoons vermouth
1 clove garlic
2 cups white wine
1 French bread, cubed

Serving: 1/8 Recipe
Protein: 15 gm
Carbs: 20 gm
Sodium: 344 mg

Calories: 238
Fat: 5.5 gm
Cholesterol: 22 mg
Calcium: 387 mg

SERVES 8

Shred cheeses. Mix cornstarch and nutmeg into vermouth. Rub a saucepan with garlic clove, pour in wine, and heat until mixture foams. Slowly stir in cheeses until melted, then whisk in cornstarch mixture. When thick, pour into fondue pot and place over burner. Use long forks to dip bread in fondue.

CHEDDAR & CHEESES

Cheddar Chutney Bites

1¼ cups grated lowfat
   Cheddar cheese
¼ cup mango chutney
¼ cup finely chopped
   pecans

MAKES 24 BITES

Mix cheese and chutney together until well blended. Roll mixture into teaspoon-sized balls about ¾ inch in diameter. Roll balls in pecans. Chill, loosely covered, at least 3 hours before serving.

Serving: 3 Bites
Protein: 15 gm
Carbs: 7 gm
Sodium: 120 mg
Calories: 146
Fat: 6.5 gm
Cholesterol: 15 mg
Calcium: 446 mg

Jalapeño Bites

2 fresh Jalapeño peppers
¾ cup grated lowfat
   Cheddar cheese
¾ cup grated lowfat
   Monterey Jack cheese
2 tablespoons fresh minced
   cilantro

MAKES 24 BITES

Seed and mince peppers. Combine peppers and cheeses in a bowl. Roll mixture into teaspoon-sized balls about ¾ inch in diameter. Roll balls in cilantro. Chill, loosely covered, at least 3 hours before serving.

Serving: 3 Bites
Protein: 15 gm
Carbs: 2 gm
Sodium: 113 mg
Calories: 101
Fat: 4 gm
Cholesterol: 15 mg
Calcium: 412 mg

CHEDDAR & CHEESES

Lemon Chèvre Dressing

2 lemons
4 oz. soft chèvre cheese
1 cup skim milk
½ cup nonfat powdered milk
1 teaspoon poppy seeds

Serving: 2 Tablespoons
Protein: 4 gm
Carbs: 5 gm
Sodium: 61 mg
Calories: 47
Fat: 2 gm
Cholesterol: 5 mg
Calcium: 88 mg

MAKES 1½ CUPS

Finely grate the rind of both lemons. Squeeze out 2 tablespoons of lemon juice. Put grated rind, juice and all other ingredients into blender, and whip until smooth. Cover, chill until ready to use.

Roquefort Dressing

½ cup nonfat cottage cheese
½ cup nonfat plain yogurt
¼ cup lowfat buttermilk
¼ cup Roquefort cheese
1 teaspoon white pepper

Serving: 2 Tablespoons
Protein: 4 gm
Carbs: 2 gm
Sodium: 120 mg
Calories: 35
Fat: 1.5 gm
Cholesterol: 6 mg
Calcium: 58 mg

MAKES 1½ CUPS

Whip cottage cheese and yogurt in blender until smooth. Add remaining ingredients and blend until smooth. Cover and refrigerate until ready to use.

CHEDDAR & CHEESES

Selecting and Storing Cheeses

Cheese should always look good. If it is cracked, discolored, wizened or just looks ugly, it probably is. Clues to look for in buying cheeses:

    Cheddar and other firm cheeses - no cracks or white mold.
    Blues and other veined cheeses - moist looking with no discoloring near rind and no black streaks in veins.
    Swiss and Parmesan - should be from Switzerland or Italy.
    Brie - glossy without a hard, cheesecake center.
    Soft ripening - plump and yielding to touch.
    Packaged cheeses - package not ripped or stuck to cheese.

Store cheeses tightly wrapped in plastic, aluminum foil or a damp cloth to prevent moisture loss. They are sensitive to smells and will pick up any strong odors. Do not store near meat, nor strong cheeses near delicate ones. Keep at 35°- 40°. The firmer the cheese, the longer its life. Parmesan and Cheddar can last months or even years under controlled conditions. Soft cheeses have shorter lives, although double and triple creams have the best holding properties, and the free flowing cheeses the shortest. Cheeses will continue to ripen, even under refrigeration, so once they have peaked in flavor, consume.

Cheese is an excellent source of calcium. Cottage, cream, mozzarella and ricotta come in nonfat varieties. Others such as Cheddar, Swiss, Colby and Muenster are available in lowfat varieties.

CHEDDAR & CHEESES

Artichoke Dip

14 oz. can artichoke hearts
  in water
4 oz. soft nonfat cream cheese
½ cup nonfat mayonnaise
¾ cup grated Parmesan
  cheese

SERVES 8

Preheat oven to 350°. Spray a small baking dish with nonstick oil. Drain artichokes, press out liquid and dice. Combine all ingredients in a mixing bowl, transfer to baking dish. Bake 25 minutes until golden on top. Serve hot.

Serving: 1/4 Recipe
Protein: 4 gm
Carbs: 9 gm
Sodium: 246 mg

Calories: 150
Fat: 11 gm
Cholesterol: 13 mg
Calcium: 112 mg

Cucumber & Feta Marinade

2 medium cucumbers
1 Vidalia or sweet onion
8 Greek olives, pitted
2 oz. feta cheese
2 tablespoons olive oil
¼ cup white wine vinegar
½ teaspoon garlic powder
½ teaspoon black pepper

SERVES 4

Peel, halve and slice cucumbers into ¼-inch-thick pieces. Halve onion and slice into thin crescents. Slice olives in half lengthwise. Combine cucumbers, onion and olives in a salad bowl. Crumble feta on top and gently toss.

In a separate bowl, mix remaining ingredients, chill about 20 minutes. Pour over salad, cover and chill 2 hours.

Serving: 1/6 Recipe
Protein: 9 gm
Carbs: 8 gm
Sodium: 558 mg

Calories: 111
Fat: 4 gm
Cholesterol: 14 mg
Calcium: 160 mg

CHEDDAR & CHEESES

Strawberry Stilton Salad

2 cups strawberries
2 tablespoons fresh chopped basil
2 tablespoons balsamic vinegar
½ teaspoon sugar
1 teaspoon canola oil
1 teaspoon water
4 cups chilled salad greens
¼ cup Stilton or other blue cheese

Serving: 1/4 Recipe
Protein: 3 gm
Carbs: 8 gm
Sodium: 124 mg
Calories: 74
Fat: 4 gm
Cholesterol: 6 mg
Calcium: 94 mg

SERVES 4

Slice strawberries into a mixing bowl, and add basil. Sprinkle vinegar and sugar over berries, toss well to coat. Chill 1 hour.

To prepare dressing, drain liquid from strawberries in to a jar. Add oil and water to jar and shake vigorously.

Arrange a cup of greens on each plate and cover greens with ½ cup strawberries and a tablespoon crumbled cheese. Drizzle each salad with strrawberry dressing. Serve immediately.

CHEDDAR & CHEESES

Broccoli Cheddar Soup

1 teaspoon canola oil
1 cup chopped onion
4 cups chopped fresh broccoli
2 cups diced peeled red potatoes
½ teaspoon garlic powder
2½ cups vegetable broth
1 bay leaf
¾ cup shredded lowfat Cheddar cheese
1 can evaporated skim milk
½ teaspoon pepper

Serving: 1/7 Recipe
Protein: 12 gm
Carbs: 26 gm
Sodium: 137 mg
Calories: 167
Fat: 2.5 gm
Cholesterol: 6 mg
Calcium: 323 mg

SERVES 7

Heat oil in soup pot and sauté onion for 5 minutes. Add 2 cups of broccoli, all of the potatoes, garlic, broth and bay leaf to pot. Bring to a boil, cover and simmer on reduced heat for 20 minutes, or until vegetables are tender.

Discard bay leaf. Remove cooked broccoli with slotted spoon. Purée half of broccoli in blender until smooth, pour back into pot. Repeat process with remaining cooked broccoli.

Add remaining 2 cups uncooked broccoli, cheese, milk and pepper to pot. Stir while cooking until broccoli is tender, about 4 minutes. Serve warm.

CHEDDAR & CHEESES

Cheddar Mornay Flounder

The mornay sauce is an excellent accompaniment to any vegetable or fish.

1½ lbs. flounder fillets

SERVES 4

Mornay Sauce - makes ¾ cup:
1 tablespoon canola oil
1 teaspoon butter
2 tablespoons flour
½ cup skim milk
3 tablespoons lowfat
   grated Cheddar cheese
pinch nutmeg
pinch paprika

Serving: 1/4 Recipe
Protein: 38 gm
Carbs: 5 gm
Sodium: 186 mg

Calories: 250
Fat: 8 gm
Cholesterol: 89 mg
Calcium: 204 mg

Poach flounder in simmering water or white wine while preparing sauce. Poach just until springy to the touch, about 12 minutes. Remove with slotted spoon.

Heat oil and butter in saucepan until foaming, then whisk in flour. Cook 2 minutes, then whisk in milk until smooth. Gradually add cheese, stirring constantly, until melted and smooth. Whisk in nutmeg and paprika.

Spoon sauce over hot fillets. Just before serving, place fish under broiler until sauce starts to brown. Serve at once.

CHEDDAR & CHEESES

Scallops with Mushrooms au Gratin

1½ cups dry vermouth
1 bay leaf
1½ lbs. scallops (whole if small, halved if large)
2 cups sliced mushrooms
1 tablespoon butter
2 tablespoons white wine
3 tablespoons flour
1 cup skim milk blended with ½ cup nonfat powdered milk
½ teaspoon white pepper
1 teaspoon lemon juice
½ cup grated lowfat Swiss Lorraine cheese

Serving: 1/6 Recipe
Protein: 26 gm
Carbs: 12 gm
Sodium: 267 mg
Calories: 213
Fat: 5.5 gm
Cholesterol: 51 mg
Calcium: 239 mg

SERVES 6

In a large saucepan, boil vermouth with bay leaf. Poach scallops with mushrooms in boiling liquid 2 minutes, cover pan, and let rest for 10 minutes. With a slotted spoon, transfer scallops and mushrooms to a bowl. Discard bay leaf. Boil poaching liquid down to 1 cup.

In another saucepan, heat butter and wine. Whisk in flour and cook 1 minute. Whisk in milk, poaching liquid and pepper. Simmer, stirring over low heat until smooth. If too thick, add a little skim milk.

Remove sauce from heat, stir in lemon juice. Fold scallops and mushrooms into sauce and transfer mixture to nonstick baking dish. Sprinkle top with cheese. Just before serving, place under broiler until top starts to brown. Serve hot.

CHEDDAR & CHEESES

Cheese Enchiladas

1 egg white
2½ cups nonfat cottage cheese
1 teaspoon canola oil
1 onion, chopped
1 garlic clove, minced
4 oz. green chiles
2 oz. black olives
15 oz. can cooked pinto beans, drained
¾ cup tomato sauce
1 tablespoon taco seasonings
1 cup lowfat Monterey Jack cheese, grated
10 oz. package corn tortillas, quartered
2 fresh tomatoes, chopped

Serving: 1/8 Recipe
Protein: 27 gm
Carbs: 40 gm
Sodium: 556 mg
Calories: 297
Fat: 4 gm
Cholesterol: 14 mg
Calcium: 250 mg

SERVES 6

Preheat oven to 350°. Spray a large baking dish with nonstick oil. In a bowl, whip egg white until stiff, then fold into 2 cups of the cottage cheese.

Heat oil in a large saucepan, then sauté onion and garlic until transparent. Chop chilies and olives, add to saucepan with beans, tomato sauce and taco seasonings. Heat for 15 minutes.

Spread one-third of the bean mixture on bottom of baking dish, cover with half of the cottage cheese mixture, half of the Jack cheese and half of the tortillas. Repeat layering process with remaining ingredients, ending with bean mixture on top. Bake 30 minutes. Serve with remaining ½ cup cottage cheese and tomatoes spread over top.

CHEDDAR & CHEESES

The Cheese Chart

TYPE/NAME	DESCRIPTION

Hard Cheeses
  Parmesan-Reggiano
  Romano
	Sweet, nutty taste, best if Italian.
	Salty flavor, from sheep's milk

Semifirm Cheeses
  Cheddar
 	
  Emmenthal/Gruyère
	English, farmhouse style is best
	In US - VT, NY, WI, OR are best
	Swiss, nutty taste, with holes

Blue Cheeses
  Roquefort (sheep's)
  Stilton
  Gorgonzola
  Danish Blue
	Grandest French, cave ripened
	English Cheddar, rivals Roquefort
	Italian, sharpens with age
	Buttery, Danish

Semisoft Cheeses
  Havarti
  Fontina
  Gouda & Edam
  Muenster
  Port-Salut
  Provolone
	Danish, mild, smooth, rindless
	Italian, nutty flavor, richer as ages
	Holland's best, mild, smooth
	Best if US, mild, light, fresh taste
	French mild, US & Danish good
	Italian, made from buffalo milk

Soft Ripening
  Brie
  Camembert
	French, luscious, creamy, US good
	French, creamy, fruity aroma

Goat/Sheep Cheeses
  Montrachet
  Feta
	French goat, best known chèvre
	Greek, salty, dry, crumbly

Special
  Liederkranz
  Limburger
  Brick
  Double/TripleCrème
  Mascarpone
	US, strong, soft ripening
	Belgian, strong, US good
	US, mild young, stronger as ages
	French, luscious, velvety
	Italian, the greatest dessert cheese

CHEDDAR & CHEESES

Risotto Parmesan

3 tablespoons minced shallots
1 tablespoon olive oil
½ cup peeled, grated carrot
1 clove garlic, minced
2 cups arborio rice
½ cup Marsala
6 cups vegetable broth
1 cup frozen peas, thawed
½ cup diced red bell pepper
2 peeled tomatoes, chopped and drained
2 teaspoons butter
1 teaspoon black pepper
½ cup fresh grated Parmesan cheese

SERVES 8 (4 AS MAIN DISH)

In a large saucepan, sauté shallots in oil. Add carrot and garlic, cook until shallots are clear. Stir in rice, increase heat to high and add Marsala. Cook until liquid is halved. Reduce heat to medium.

In a separate pot, bring vegetable broth to a boil. Add hot broth to rice, ½ cup at a time. Stir and allow rice to absorb liquid after each addition. Some liquid should remain after final addition. Add peas, pepper and tomatoes, then cook another 5 minutes. Add more boiling broth if needed to make rice creamy and soft. Just before serving, stir in butter, pepper and grated Parmesan.

Serving: 1/8 Recipe
Protein: 9 gm
Carbs: 58 gm
Sodium: 180 mg
Calories: 337
Fat: 4.5 gm
Cholesterol: 9 mg
Calcium: 95 mg

CHEDDAR & CHEESES

Cheesy Macaroni with Roasted Vegetables

3 cups peeled and diced eggplant
2 cups sliced mushrooms
1 cup chopped red bell pepper
1 cup chopped yellow pepper
1 cup chopped zucchini
4 garlic cloves, minced
2 teaspoons canola oil
½ cup flour
2¾ cups skim milk
¾ cup shredded lowfat provolone cheese
¾ cup fresh grated Parmesan cheese
¼ teaspoon black pepper
6 cups cooked elbow macaroni

SERVES 8

Preheat oven to 450°. Spray a large shallow baking pan with nonstick oil. Toss 5 vegetables, garlic and oil in baking pan. Bake 30 minutes, turning occasionally until browned. Remove pan from oven and set aside. Reduce oven temperature to 375°.

In a large saucepan, whisk flour into milk until blended. Cook, stirring constantly, until thickened. Add provolone, ½ cup Parmesan and pepper, stirring until cheese melts. Mix macaroni into cheese sauce, then pour over vegetables. Sprinkle remaining Parmesan over top, bake 20 minutes, or until bubbly.

Serving: 1/8 Recipe
Protein: 24 gm
Carbs: 96 gm
Sodium: 214 mg
Calories: 548
Fat: 8 gm
Cholesterol: 17 mg
Calcium: 314 mg

CHEDDAR & CHEESES

Onion Pie

SERVES 6

- 1 egg white
- 2 cups chopped onions
- 2 teaspoons canola oil
- 2 eggs, beaten
- 2 egg whites, beaten
- 1 cup skim milk
- ¼ cup nonfat dry powdered milk
- 1 teaspoon Worcestershire sauce
- ½ cup grated Gruyère cheese

Preheat oven to 375°. Spray a 9-inch pie plate with nonstick oil. Lightly beat single egg white, then brush it over the bottom and sides of the pie plate.

Sauté onions in oil until nearly clear. In a mixing bowl, beat together eggs and whites, milks and Worcestershire sauce. Stir in grated cheese and sautéed onions. Pour into pie plate. Bake 30 minutes, or until golden brown. Serve warm, or chill for a delicious cold picnic lunch.

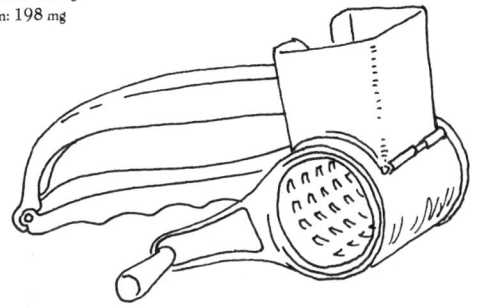

Serving: 1 Piece
Protein: 10 gm
Carbs: 9 gm
Sodium: 125 mg
Calories: 130
Fat: 6.5 gm
Cholesterol: 82 mg
Calcium: 198 mg

CHEDDAR & CHEESES

Gorgonzola Potatoes

4 large baking potatoes, scrubbed and dried
1 tablespoon butter
2 cloves garlic, minced
½ cup nonfat sour cream
2 oz. Gorgonzola or other blue cheese
1 tablespoon minced fresh parsley
1 tablespoon minced fresh chives
½ teaspoon paprika

Serving: 1/4 Recipe
Protein: 8 gm
Carbs: 41 gm
Sodium: 263 mg
Calories: 261
Fat: 7.5 gm
Cholesterol: 19 mg
Calcium: 129 mg

SERVES 4

Preheat oven to 375°. Pierce potatoes all over with a fork. Bake 75 minutes.

Melt butter in saucepan, and lightly sauté garlic 2 minutes. Do not brown.

Remove potatoes from oven when done, cool, cut a slit lengthwise in each potato, and scoop out into a bowl, keeping skins intact. Reserve potato skins.

Mash potatoes with a fork, then add garlic butter, sour cream, blue cheese, parsley and chives. Mix thoroughly and put potato mixture back into potato skins. Sprinkle tops with paprika. Arrange on a baking sheet and bake for 15 minutes. Serve hot from the oven.

CHEDDAR & CHEESES

Brie Pudding with Fruit Sauce

¾ cup dried apricots
2 cups peeled peaches,
   fresh or canned
1 cup apricot nectar
1 tablespoon honey
1 tablespoon lime juice
5 oz. Brie cheese
8 cups stale white or
   French bread, cubed
2 tablespoons brown sugar
12 oz. can evaporated
   skim milk
pinch of salt
2 egg whites, beaten
2 eggs, beaten

Serving: 1/9 Recipe
Protein: 11 gm
Carbs: 32 gm
Sodium: 178 mg
Calories: 216
Fat: 6 gm
Cholesterol: 64 mg
Calcium: 173 mg

SERVES 9

Preheat oven to 350°. Spray a 9-inch square baking dish with nonstick oil.

For fruit sauce, dice apricots and peaches. In a saucepan, boil fruits in nectar. Cover pan and let rest 30 minutes. Drain, reserving 2 tablespoons nectar. In a bowl, gently stir fruits, nectar, honey and juice.

Remove and discard rind from Brie. Cut Brie into tiny pieces. Arrange half of the bread cubes in baking dish. Cover with half of the Brie. Sprinkle with half of the brown sugar. Repeat process.

In separate bowl, combine milk, salt and eggs. Pour mixture over bread cubes. Cover and chill 30 minutes. Bake for 35 minutes or until inserted knife comes out clean. Serve warm with fruit sauce spread evenly over top of each serving.

CHEDDAR & CHEESES

Blueberry Mascarpone Cheesecake

cheesecloth
1 coeur à la crème mold
12 oz. mascarpone cheese
6 oz. farmer cheese
6 oz. nonfat cream cheese
3 tablespoons powdered sugar
1 cup evaporated skim milk
½ cup nonfat dry powdered milk
4 cups blueberries
½ cup sugar
2 tablespoons red wine vinegar
¼ teaspoon cinnamon
¼ teaspoon nutmeg
pinch of mace
pinch of ground cloves

Serving: 1/10 Recipe
Protein: 14 gm
Carbs: 29 gm
Sodium: 416 mg
Calories: 263
Fat: 11.5 gm
Cholesterol: 31 mg
Calcium: 332 mg

MAKES 10-PIECE CHEESECAKE

Dampen cheesecloth, thoroughly wring out and use it to line the 8-inch coeur à la crème mold, with enough cheesecloth remaining outside to cover top.

Process all 3 cheeses and sugar in food processor until smooth. In a measuring cup, mix evaporated and dry milk. With blender running, add milk, process 1 minute. Fill mold with cheese mixture, cover with cheesecloth, and set mold into a larger pan. Chill 24 hours.

Heat blueberries and all remaining ingredients in a saucepan over medium heat for 15 minutes, stirring frequently. Raise heat and boil 5 minutes. Reduce heat to a simmer for 10 minutes. Cool and chill at least 2 hours.

To serve, invert mold over plate, remove cheesecloth and surround with sauce.

CHEDDAR & CHEESES

Tiramisu Parfaits
A dessert to splurge!

1 egg yolk
1 egg
2 tablespoons powdered sugar
2 tablespoons Grand Marnier liqueur
1 tablespoon sweet Marsala
8 oz. mascarpone cheese
6 tablespoons cold espresso coffee
18 plain ladyfingers, broken into thirds
2 oz. grated milk chocolate

Serving: 1/8 Recipe
Protein: 6 gm
Carbs: 55 gm
Sodium: 247 mg
Calories: 330
Fat: 9.5 gm
Cholesterol: 94 mg
Calcium: 82 mg

SERVES 8

With electric beaters, beat eggs and powdered sugar until pale yellow. Add a tablespoon each of the Grand Marnier and Marsala. Beat in mascarpone until mixture is thick and smooth.

In a separate bowl, combine 1 tablespoon Grand Marnier and coffee.

Place 3 pieces of the broken ladyfingers into each of 8 large wine glasses. Drizzle half of the coffee liquid over ladyfingers in glasses. Spoon half the mascarpone mixture over ladyfingers. Sprinkle half of the grated chocolate over the mascarpone. Repeat the layering process with remaining ingredients. Chill at least 3 hours before serving.

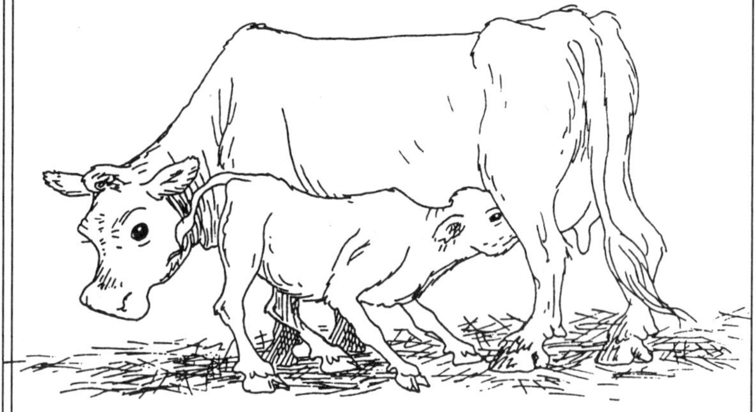